Variable Star Quilts
and How to Make Them

Marsha McCloskey & Nancy J. Martin

Dover Publications, Inc., New York

in association with

Published in Canada by General Publishing Company, Ltd., 30 Lesmill Road,
Don Mills, Toronto, Ontario.
Published in the United Kingdom by Constable and Company, Ltd., 3 The
Lanchesters, 162–164 Fulham Palace Road, London W6 9ER.

Bibliographical Note

This Dover edition, first published in 1995, is an unabridged republication of
A Dozen Variables, originally published by That Patchwork Place, Bothell,
Washington, in 1987.

Library of Congress Cataloging-in-Publication Data

McCloskey, Marsha.
   [Dozen variables]
   Variable star quilts and how to make them / Marsha McCloskey & Nancy
Martin.
      p.   cm.
   Originally published: A dozen variables. Bothell, Wash. : That Patchwork
Place, 1987.
   Includes bibliographical references.
   ISBN 0-486-28595-2
   1. Patchwork—Patterns. 2. Patchwork quilts. I. Martin, Nancy
J. II. Title.
TT835.M2743 1995
746.46—dc20   94-41222
                                                  CIP

Manufactured in the United States of America
Dover Publications, Inc., 31 East 2nd Street, Mineola, N.Y. 11501

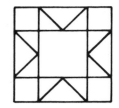

ACKNOWLEDGMENTS

Special thanks are extended to:

Trudie Hughes, Carolann Palmer, Nancy Mahoney, Christine Russell and Suzanne Keeney Lucy for the use of their quilts.

Sharon Yenter, In the Beginning Quilts, for the use of her Variable Star quilt for photography.

Freda Smith for her fine quilting.

Georgina Fries for her quilting service.

Roberta Horton, *Calico and Beyond: The Use Of Patterned Fabric in Quilts,* and Judy Martin, *Patchworkbook,* whose work is partially reproduced here.

CREDITS

Photography . . . . Carl Murray
Skip Howard Photos
Illustration and Graphics . . . . Stephanie Benson
Chris A. Lassen

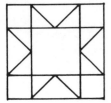

PREFACE

Two basic types of star designs appear in patchwork. Le Moyne Stars consist of true diamonds and have equidistant points, while grid-based stars are made up of squares and triangles. Variable Star is the name given to the basic drafting for all grid-based stars. It is a simple design, easy to piece, and extremely useful in its many variations.

I chose a simplified version of the classic Variable Star, known as the Sawtooth Star, as the basis for four quilt tops that I made in the summer of 1985. All multi-fabric quilts, my star series became the samples for a Scrap Quilts class that I taught in Seattle. Taking the Variable or Sawtooth Star as a starting place, students were to experiment with colorings and sets to design and produce multi-fabric quilts. The resulting quilts were visually complex, yet simple in concept and construction.

Nancy Martin, friend and publisher, was so taken with the quilts as a group, both mine and the students', that she encouraged the development of this book. She actually pieced so many of the quilt designs herself, that we decided to collaborate on the project. This book is the result. I hope you share our enthusiasm as you use this workbook to create your own designs and Variable Star quilts.

Marsha McCloskey

CONTENTS

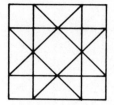

"Among the heavenly bodies those known as variables are so called because they show distinct changes in brightness from time to time; so in patchwork, accent in coloring gave to this much-used and easily assembled pattern a versatility which led to its apt name."

Florence Peto, Antiques, *July 1942*

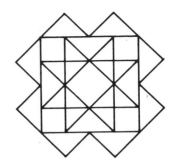

INTRODUCTION

This book has been planned as a workbook to help you create your own Variable Star quilt designs. The first section of the book contains a history of the Variable Star block, followed by a quilt planning section with tips on fabric selection, color, and quilt design.

The pattern section of this book begins on page 16. Quilts are grouped according to the design approach and share common templates at the end of this section. Color photographs, design worksheets, fabric requirements, and complete step-by-step directions are given for each quilt. Also included in this section is a Glossary of Techniques, which gives tips and instructions on all phases of quiltmaking.

Begin by reading the entire book to get a general idea of the designs and techniques covered. Skim, if you are anxious to get started, but do take the time to familiarize yourself with the design process.

Choosing only a dozen quilts for this book was difficult, since this versatile pattern and design technique allow the creation of seemingly endless variations. We encourage you to proceed beyond our twelve patterns to create your own wonderful Variable Stars.

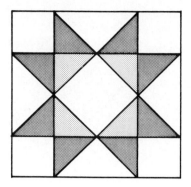

Variable Star

Dolly Madison Star

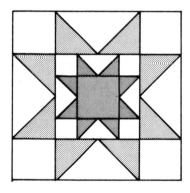

Rising Star

Ohio Star

HISTORY

As an astronomical term, a variable star is one that varies in its magnitude due to internal changes or to external causes, such as an eclipse by a dark companion. What a fitting name for this versatile block that varies according to its coloration or the coloration of its companion block.

The Variable Star is one of the oldest quilt patterns, appearing in America during the last quarter of the 18th century. Women often designed symbolic quilt patterns, so chosing a star for a quilt design was inevitable.

Stars have always been symbols of high ideals and hopes. They are often in emblems, flags, and mottoes. "Hitch your wagon to a star" was an 18th-century expression encouraging one to set high goals and then work hard to reach them.

Stars often are used as religious symbols. The star of Bethlehem is a symbol of Christianity—no Christmas tree is complete without a shining star. The six-pointed star of David is the symbol of the Jewish faith.

Stars often appeared in the folklore, legends, and religions of primitive people and the ancients. There is a lovely Blackfoot Indian legend about the Morning Star. Ancient peoples sometimes worshipped the stars as gods.

Many have speculated about the origin of the Variable Star block. Jonathan Holstein, in *The Pieced Quilt: An American Design Tradition*, supposes that such a design is invented over and over again by artisans who begin with the square as a basis of a pieced design. Of the Variable Star he writes, "(it) can be found in Roman and Arabic mosaic floors and architectural decoration, Renaissance decorative inlay, marquetry on furniture, and the like, (its) sustained popularity due to the convenience of working with the divisions of the square in techniques which require piecing together parts of contrasting colors."

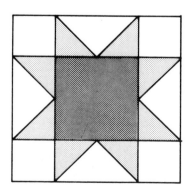

Sawtooth Star
Evening Star

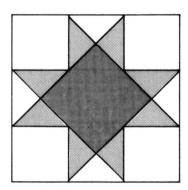

Texas Star
Lone Star

European influences are strong in American patchwork. English catalogs and quilting books refer to the Variable Star as The Evening Star. Choice examples made from large-scale chintz patterns, popular in the 1800's, have survived. Perhaps the name Evening Star was inspired by the aria "Evening Star" from Richard Wagner's opera, *Tannhauser,* written in 1845.

The Variable Star block was usually seen as the corner block in New England medallion-style quilts. An exception is the undated Virginia patchwork quilt, Pinwheel, attributed to Martha Washington. In this quilt, four Variable Star blocks are found in the corners of an inner border.

It was not until the early 1800's that the Variable Star pattern was used as the main quilt block, rather than as a border element. Early glazed linsey-woolsey quilts made in two bright solid colors still survive.

The cotton quilts made during this time period often combined a multitude of prints for the star with a rich, bright, large-scale chintz for the alternate blocks. Large-scale chintzs also were used in borders to give interest and depth to quilts. The Shelburne Museum in Shelburne, Vermont, contains an excellent example of this type of quilt, which is signed and dated in black cross stitch: E.L.H., 1839.

As our country grew and variations of the original Variable Star block appeared, the name of the block changed. In the early 1800's a Variable Star with a pieced center variation was named Dolly Madison, after the popular White House hostess. Dolly Madison Star generally used two prints: a dark star set against a light background.

By 1840, when William Henry Harrison was running for the presidency under the slogan "Tippecanoe and Tyler Too," the original Variable Star pattern took on a new set and used the slogan for its name. In this set, the Variable Stars are sewn together in long, vertical strips, which are then combined with rows of solid strips in the English "strippie" style.

The Variable Star was the name used for the block in the East, especially in New England. A variation called Rising Star, featuring a star within the star center, originated in Upstate New York in the first quarter of the 19th century. As the pattern moved westward, it became known as the Ohio Star. Ohio Star was usually constructed as a light-colored star on a dark background.

A variation of the Variable Star block, without the contrasting center diamond, was referred to as the Sawtooth Star. The saw was an ever-present tool in pioneer days, used to clear land as settlers moved west. Quilt borders of contrasting triangles resembled these long saws and were called Sawtooth borders. The Sawtooth pattern was probably devised by a quilter working with contrasting triangular shapes.

"Tippecanoe and Tyler Too"

When our country became involved with the question of Texas annexation in 1844, the Variable Star became known as the Texas Star or the Lone Star. Other variations of the Variable Star include Western Star, Star of Hope, and Star of the West.

Just as the Variable Star block changed, so did the setting arrangement of the blocks. The Variable Star was usually set with unpieced alternate blocks, either straight or on the diagonal, until 1870-1880. At this time, several Variable Star quilts were set with sashing (with or without setting squares) and some Variable Stars used zigzag sashing.

Variable Star Quilt, origin unknown, c. 1840, 85" x 83 1/2". Early printed cottons are used with striped sashing and borders in this Variable Star quilt top. (Collection of Sharon Yenter, In the Beginning Quilts, Seattle, Washington)

QUILT PLANNING

QUILT SIZE

The size of your quilt will depend on its intended function. You will need a quilt plan before you can buy fabric and begin sewing. A quilt plan can be a scale drawing of a quilt design on 1/8" graph paper. From such a plan, it is easy to tell the number of blocks and set pieces that will be needed to complete a given quilt, as well as finished dimensions of plain borders. Twelve quilt plans for Variable Star quilts are provided in the pattern section. To make existing quilt plans larger or smaller, add or subtract blocks, set pieces, or borders until the desired size is reached.

DESIGN

The charactor of your quilt will depend on both your fabric selection and design choices. No other quilter has been where you have been, made the same choices, bought the same fabrics. Your fabric collection is unique, and your quilt will be too.

Stardancer, by Nancy Martin, 1985, Woodinville, Washington, 52" x 74". A lively collection of prints is surrounded by a paisley border. Quilted by Freda Smith.

Stardancer, by Marsha McCloskey, 1985, Seattle, Washington, 52" x 74". The same color recipe made with a different fabric collection.

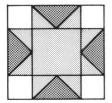 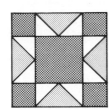

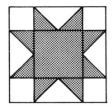 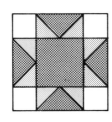

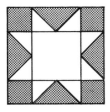 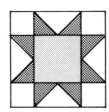

Many of the quilts presented in this book are scrap or multi-fabric quilts. Working with many fabrics expands color and shading possibilities and makes the star blocks even more versatile.

After studying the quilts in this book, you probably will have a good idea of which quilt you want to make. The easiest way to proceed is to use an existing quilt plan. The quilt plans provided in the pattern section of this book include templates, color suggestions, fabric requirements, and step-by-step instructions. If you prefer to create your own quilt designs using the star blocks, read this section over. Start your own quilt design from scratch as described here, or incorporate some of the suggestions in the quilt plans provided later in the book.

This star series evolved over two years of sketching, making quilts, and teaching classes based on the Variable Star. The star we have worked with most often in this book is a simplified version of the Variable Star called the Sawtooth Star. Some of the quilts were designed and made by the students as a result of some class exercises. Before selecting your fabric, take the time to experiment with these design exercises.

In the first exercise, derived from *Calico and Beyond: the Use of Patterned Fabric in Quilts* by Roberta Horton, students were to experiment with different placements of light, medium, and dark tones in the basic Variable Star or Sawtooth Star block. Changing color emphasis this way illustrates how the look of the block can be changed without altering basic shapes or their placement.

The next exercise, derived from the *Patchworkbook* by Judy Martin, involved combining the basic star block with alternate pieced blocks to form overall quilt designs. The idea of using two blocks to form an overall pattern is actually an old one. Several classic quilt designs use this idea: Snowball, consisting of Snowball and Nine Patch blocks, and Evening Star, made up of Snowball and Evening Star blocks. Students were to make line drawings of star blocks alternating with simple pieced blocks of the same size. They were invited to add new lines to their designs or to drop out some lines and look for any secondary designs that might appear during the process. Once an interesting line drawing evolved, it was to be shaded with colored pencils to bring out the most interesting aspect of the design. We were not looking necessarily for quilt colors, but for placement of light, medium, and dark tones.

If you want to try this exercise, use the worksheet on page 52 to see what new designs and shading variations you can discover. Six of the quilts in the pattern section are designs formed by combining **the star with an alternate pieced block. Many more are possible, using the 8" blocks provided.**

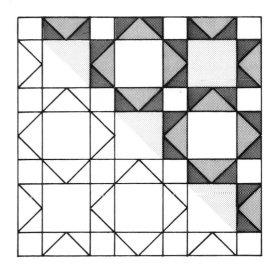

SHADING

Begin with a line drawing of a quilt design. Use one provided here or one you have drawn yourself. Study the line drawing. What do you see? Are secondary designs created where the blocks meet? Can these forms be emphasized by coloring or shading?

Even though a quilt may be constructed in unit blocks, the block boundaries can be ignored for coloring purposes. The Blazing Sawtooth quilt and Jane's Quilt variation on page 32 are good examples of two very different quilt designs derived from the same line drawing.

While you are coloring, experiment with different arrangements of light, medium, and dark tones. Keep in mind that these are relative terms. How a fabric is finally defined depends on the fabrics around it. Medium tones are especially changeable. They can be light when placed next to a dark fabric or dark when put next to a very light one. Sketch until you develop a light and dark relationship that seems to work. Then try it with fabric.

FABRIC SELECTION

To select your fabrics, begin with a color idea or theme. Though another quilt may inspire you, many times a single fabric will provide the key inspiration for color in a quilt. This main fabric or idea print will give you color clues as to what other fabrics will go with it. Think in terms of related colors and contrasts. If your idea print is dark, choose something light in a related color to go with it. When two fabrics are side by side, there should be a definite line where one stops and the other begins to show contrast.

Contrast, both in color and visual texture, makes pieced designs more visible. Visual texture is the way a print looks—is it spotty, smooth, plain, dappled, linear, rhythmical, or swirly? Are the figures far apart or close together? Mix large prints with small prints, flowery allover designs with linear rhythmical prints. Too many similar prints can create a dull surface or one that is visually confusing.

For best results, select lightweight, closely woven, 100 percent cotton fabrics. Polyester content may make small patchwork pieces difficult to cut and sew accurately. Preshrink all fabrics before use. Wash light and dark colors separately with regular laundry detergent and warm water. If you suspect a dark color might run, rinse it separtely in plain warm water until the water remains clear. Dry fabrics in the dryer and press them well before cutting.

The 100 percent cotton ideal is not always possible with quilts created from fabric collections of long-standing. Some of my most interesting prints were purchased before I followed the 100 percent rule—they are polyester/cotton blends of uncertain content. I know I shouldn't use them, but the colors and prints are unobtainable today and often serve a unique design purpose in the quilt.

COLOR RECIPE

Define a color recipe for your design. What color will be the dark? What the light? A simple recipe would be to use a constant background fabric in all the blocks and to make the design motif in different scrap fabrics. Another recipe would be to change the background fabric in each block as well. This inconsistency adds depth and movement to the simplest quilt designs.

Having chosen a tentative color recipe based on your color theme and shaded sketches, select a range of fabrics for each color group in the recipe. If black is one of the colors, pick several black prints in differing intensities and visual textures. Pull every black in your collection that even remotely fits the criteria. Not all of these will be used, but it is important to study the possibilities. Do the same with each color group in the recipe.

Resist overmatching colors and textures. Use all types of prints. As a color group, reds can range from rust to red to maroon to brown and still occupy the same position in the block design. A group of lights can go from a very white to ecru to medium tones. Darks can range from very dark to medium. If your color grouping looks boring, throw in a color surprise, a non sequitur—navy in a run of browns or true red where only shades of maroon and rust have been used.

FABRIC SKETCH

Once you have chosen a quilt design, an arrangement of lights and darks, and pulled runs of fabric from your collection, the next step is to make a fabric sketch. This trial run of blocks, or block segments, will test your color recipe (the projected color arrangement).

Cut the pieces for one or more blocks from your chosen fabrics. Place the shapes on a piece of needlepunch or flannel, which has been hung on the wall, to evaluate the effect. Cut more pieces and make changes until it pleases you. When the color arrangment is set, piece the blocks. Now, cut and sew more blocks in the same recipe. Make needed color and design changes as the quilt grows.

Feel free to experiment with different prints and color arrangements. Push yourself; be adventurous. Go beyond what you consider safe fabric and color usage. Break a few rules. Forget about centering large motifs; cabbage roses and other large prints work better when they are cut randomly. Stripes and plaids can be cut randomly, too—even off-grain if you wish. Try using the wrong side of some prints to get just the right tone. If you make a mistake in piecing, consider leaving it in to create interest. If you run out of one fabric, substitute another and keep going.

Northwest Star, designed by Marsha Mc-Closkey, 1985, Seattle, Washington, 84" x 84". A raffle quilt completed by parents, teachers, and friends of the Northwest School of the Arts, Humanities, and Environment to benefit the scholarship fund.

VARYING CONTRASTS

One strategy for making quilts visually interesting is to vary the contrast in the unit blocks. High contrast blocks are needed to establish the design, but more interest will be created when the other blocks in the quilt have lower contrast. It's okay to lose the design in some parts of the quilt. The viewer expects the same design to be regularly repeated and will search for a "disappearing" design motif to make sure it is there.

Background fabrics are particularly important in creating variations in the contrast of the blocks. Bright whites can hold the same design spaces in blocks as ecru and more medium tones. The whites will add sparkle to the quilt and lead the eye from one part to the next. Yellow, used in small amounts is, like bright white, a real eye-catcher, creating movement wherever it appears.

SETS

If you are designing your own quilt rather than using one of the twelve patterns provided, try out several block arrangements or sets before you sew the blocks together.

Blocks can be set straight-on or on the diagonal. Some look best side by side; others look best separated by alternate blocks or lattices. Combine Variable Stars with another block, such as Attic Windows, for a unique set. Take time to play with your blocks and arrange them in different ways. Vary spatial relationships. Original quilt plans sometimes need changing, so don't be afraid to do so.

The coloring of the set pieces, alternate blocks, or lattices is a very important part of the quilt's total look. Set pieces that are the same color as the background of the unit blocks will float the design, while those cut from contrasting fabric will outline each block and emphasize its squareness.

BORDERS

Most of the quilts in the pattern section have simple wide borders. Using these borders is the easiest and most effective way to contain all the movement present when using multi-print fabrics, which may form both overall and secondary patterns on the quilt top.

You may wish to experiment with other variations on your quilt drawing. Multiple borders or striped fabric, which has been mitered at the corners, would be another possibility.

Star Dreams Through Attic Windows, designed by Marsha McCloskey, 1984, Seattle, Washington, 80" x 90". A raffle quilt completed by parents, teachers, and friends of the Northwest School of the Arts, Humanities, and Environment to benefit the scholarship fund.

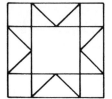

QUILT PATTERNS

Twelve complete quilt plans are provided in this section of the book. These plans include color suggestions, fabric requirements, step-by-step directions, and quilt drawings.

The quilts are composed of 8" blocks and share templates, lattices, and set pieces, which are found on pages 53-57. Yardage, dimensions, complete directions and diagrams, and templates are given for each quilt.

Measurements for patterns and borders include 1/4" seam allowance. Cutting directions are given for one block only; multiply by the number of blocks you are making to determine complete cutting specifications. Cutting directions for set pieces and pieced borders are for the entire quilt.

Consult the Glossary of Techniques on pages 58-63 for piecing diagrams, assembly methods, and complete directions on quilt-making techniques. The first six quilt designs, Oklahoma Star, Ohio Star, Shoo Fly Star, Rising Star, Road to Oklahoma, and Blazing Sawtooth, are formed by combining two alternate pieced blocks.

Checkerboard Stars and Stardancer are two quilt designs where the Variable Star block is combined with lattice segments. Rock Star, Starlight, and Star Chase are constructed by piecing block segments. When these segments are pieced together, a Variable Star, as well as a secondary design, emerges. The remaining quilt design, Twinkling Stars, is made from identical blocks. When the blocks are sewn next to each other, the small "twinkling stars" appear.

Partially shaded line drawings accompany each quilt design. Use these drawings as worksheets and experiment with various colors and shadings, so you can make the quilt designs even more individual.

Oklahoma Star, by Marsha McCloskey, 1985, Seattle, Washington, 53" x 76". Fabrics from the 1970's are combined with overdyed prints in a diagonal set to create a lively quilt top. Quilted by Freda Smith.

Vanilla Fudge, by Nancy Martin, 1985, Woodinville, Washington, 50 1/2" x 50 1/2". This version of the Oklahoma Star features solid color stars with "cabbage rose" centers set against a swirling background print. Background fabric replaces the pieced half and quarter blocks. Anonymous quilter.

Alternating Pieced Blocks

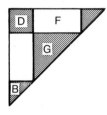

Sawtooth Star   Puss In A Corner

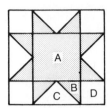
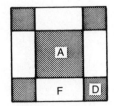

Half block   Quarter block

Dimensions: 53 3/4" x 76"

Measurements for patterns and borders include 1/4" seam allowance

Materials: 45" wide yardage

Light fabric: 1 1/4 yds. assorted white, beige, tan prints
Medium fabric: 1 1/2 yds. assorted gold, rust prints
Dark fabric: 1 1/2 yds. assorted brown prints
Border: 2 yds. brown fabric
Backing: 3 1/4 yds. fabric
Batting, binding and thread to finish

Cutting:

Sawtooth Star:
    A: Cut 1 medium
    B: Cut 8 medium
    C: Cut 4 light
    D: Cut 4 light

Puss In A Corner:
    A: Cut 1 dark
    D: Cut 4 dark
    F: Cut 4 light

Half Blocks:
    B: Cut 2 dark
    D: Cut 1 dark
    F: Cut 2 light
    G: Cut 1 dark

Quarter Blocks:
    B: Cut 2 dark
    C: Cut 1 dark
    F: Cut 1 light

Directions:

1. Cut and piece 24 Sawtooth Star blocks.

2. Cut and piece 15 Puss In A Corner blocks

3. Cut and piece 4 quarter blocks and 16 half blocks.

4. Set together top as shown, alternating Sawtooth Star and Puss In A Corner blocks, using half blocks and quarter blocks to complete diagonal rows.

5. Stitch 4 1/2" x 68 1/2" borders to each side.

6. Stitch 4 1/2" x 53 3/4" borders to top and bottom of quilt top.

7. Add batting and backing, then quilt or tie.

8. Bind with bias strips.

Variation:
VANILLA FUDGE

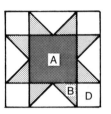
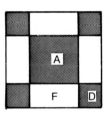

Sawtooth Star   Puss In A Corner

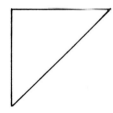

Set Piece 1   Set Piece 2

Dimensions: 50 1/2" x 50 1/2"

Set Pieces 1 and 2 are substituted for the pieced half and quarter blocks. Cut from background fabric to float the design.

Dimensions: 53" x 76"

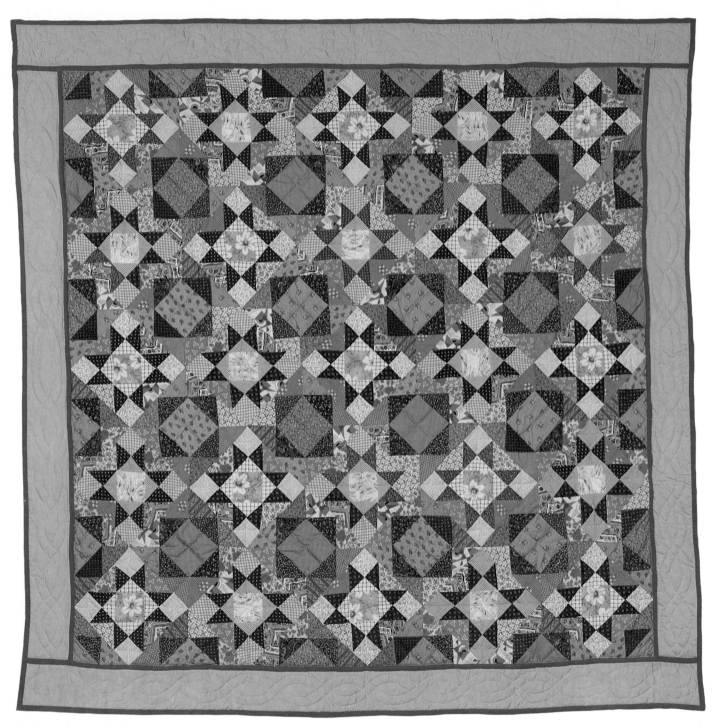

30's and 80's Quilt, by Carolann Palmer, 1985, Seattle, Washington, 64 1/2'' x 64 1/2''. Using fabric from the 1930's and 1980's, Carolann has created many secondary designs in this Ohio Star quilt.

Dimensions: 64 1/2'' x 64 1/2''

Alternating Pieced Blocks

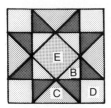 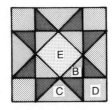

Variable Star   Variable Star
Coloration A   Coloration B

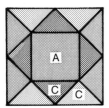

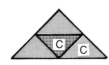

Economy   Quarter Block

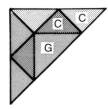 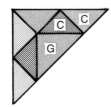

Half Blocks

Dimensions: 64 1/2" x 64 1/2"
Measurements for patterns and borders include 1/4" seam allowance.

Materials: 45 inch wide yardage

Light fabric: 1 yd. assorted light green prints
Medium fabric: 1 yd. assorted light pink prints
Accent fabric 1: 1 1/2 yds. assorted cranberry prints
Accent fabric 2: 1 1/2 yds. medium green prints
Dark fabric: 1 1/2 yds. dark green
Borders: 1 7/8 yds. light green fabric
Backing: 3 3/4 yds. fabric
Batting, binding and thread to finish

Cutting:

Variable Star
Coloration A
  B: Cut 4 light
    Cut 8 dark
  C: Cut 4 medium
  D: Cut 4 light
  E. Cut 1 medium

Variable Star
Coloration B
  B: Cut 4 medium
    Cut 8 dark
  C: Cut 4 medium
  D: Cut 4 medium
  E: Cut 1 light

Economy:
  A: Cut 1 accent fabric 2
  C: Cut 4 light
    Cut 4 medium
    Cut 4 accent fabric 1

Half Block:
  G: Cut 1 accent fabric 2
  C: Cut 2 medium
    Cut 2 accent fabric 1
    Cut 2 accent fabric 2

Quarter Block:
  C: Cut 3 accent fabric 2
    Cut 1 accent fabric 1

Directions:

1. Cut and piece 25 Variable Star blocks, 13 from coloration A and 12 from coloration B.

2. Cut and piece 16 Economy blocks, 16 half blocks (8 of each coloration) and 4 quarter blocks.

3. Set together top as shown, alternating Economy and Variable Star blocks, using half blocks and quarter blocks to complete diagonal rows.

4. Stitch 4 1/4" x 57" borders to each side.

5. Stitch 4 1/4" x 64 1/2" borders to top and bottom of quilt top.

6. Add batting and backing, then quilt or tie.

7. Bind with bias strips.

Alternating Pieced Blocks

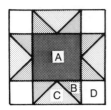 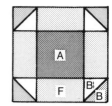

Sawtooth Star   Shoo Fly

Dimensions: 40" x 56"

Measurements for patterns and borders include 1/4" seam allowance.

Materials: 45" wide yardage

Light fabric: 1 1/4 yds. assorted white, beige, tan prints
Medium fabric: 1 yd. assorted gray prints
Accent fabric: 1/2 yd. assorted tan prints
Dark fabric: 1 yd. assorted navy, red, maroon, rust, burgundy prints
Backing: 1 3/4 yds. fabric
Batting, binding, and thread to finish

Cutting:

Sawtooth Star:
   A: Cut 1 dark
   B: Cut 8 medium
   C: Cut 4 accent
   D: Cut 4 light

Shoofly:
   A: Cut 1 dark
   B: Cut 4 light
      Cut 4 medium
   F: Cut 4 accent

Directions:

1. Cut and piece 17 Sawtooth Star blocks.

2. Cut and piece 18 Shoo Fly blocks.

3. Set together top, alternating Sawtooth Star and Shoo Fly blocks.

4. Add batting and backing, then quilt or tie.

5. Bind with bias strips.

Variation:

EVENING STAR

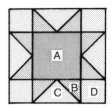 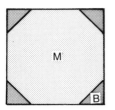

Sawtooth Star   Snowball

Dimensions: 40" x 40"

An Evening Star quilt can be made by substituting the Snowball block for the Shoo Fly block.

First Star, By Christine Russell, 1986, Seattle, Washington, 40" x 56". A lovely overall pattern emerges when the Sawtooth Star and Shoo Fly are combined.

Evening Star, by Trudie Hughes, 1986, Elm Grove, Wisconsin, 40" x 40". This variation, created by substituting the Snowball block for the Shoo Fly block, allows room for a delicate quilting design. Striped fabric creates an effective border to frame the design.

Dimensions: 40" x 56"

Alternating Pieced Blocks

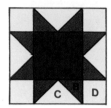   

Sawtooth Star   Square Within A Square

Dimensions: 55" x 78"
Measurements for patterns and borders include 1/4" seam allowance.

Materials: 45" wide yardage
Light fabric: 1 3/8 yds. beige print
Medium fabric: 1 yd. rust print
Dark fabric: 2 yds. navy print
Border fabric: 2 yds. for a simple border
(For multiple border you will need 3/4 yd. for first border or 2 1/2 yds. if using a border stripe, 1/2 yd. for second border, and 7/8 yd. for outside border.)
Backing: 3 yards
Batting, binding, and thread to finish

Cutting:
Sawtooth Star:
  A: Cut 1 dark
  B: Cut 8 medium
  C: Cut 4 light
  D: Cut 4 light

Square Within A Square:
  G: Cut 4 dark
  K: Cut 1 light

Set pieces for entire quilt:
  Set Piece 1: Cut 4 dark
  Set Piece 2: Cut 16 dark

Directions:
1. The "Rising Star" quilt pictured has multiple borders: one is a striped fabric (you can choose to use a non-stripe in this position); the other two are prints. The corners are mitered. Cut the border strips and sew them together to form border units. (See "Mitering Corners" on page 61.)

First Border:
  Cut two 2" × 56" strips
  Cut two 2" × 79" strips
Second Border:
  Cut two 1 1/2" × 56" strips
  Cut two 1 1/2" × 79" strips
Outside Border:
  Cut two 3" × 56" strips
  Cut two 3" × 79" strips

2. Cut 16 Set Piece 2 and 4 Set Piece 1 from dark fabric.

3. Cut and piece 24 Sawtooth Star blocks and 15 Square Within A Square blocks.

4. Set together blocks as pictured.

5. Add borders and miter corners.

6. Add batting and backing, then quilt or tie.

7. Bind with bias strips.

Rising Star, by Marsha McCloskey, 1982, Seattle, Washington, 55" x 78". Quilted by Nancy Dice.

Dimensions: 55'' x 78''

Variation I:

AMISH RISING STAR

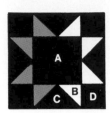 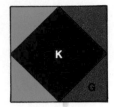

Sawtooth Star   Square Within A Square

Dimensions: 41" x 41"

A variation of the Rising Star executed in Amish colors.

Amish Rising Star, by Suzanne Kenney Lucy, 1986, Deming, Washington, 41" x 41". A variation of the Rising Star executed in Amish colors.

Variation II:
DIAMOND GIRL

   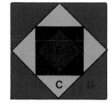

Sawtooth Star   Diamond Girl

Dimensions: 48" x 64"

The Diamond Girl quilt combines the Sawtooth Star and Diamond Girl blocks in a straight set.

Diamond Girl, by Nancy Martin, 1987, Woodinville, Washington, 48" x 64". This variation of the Rising Star pattern combines the Diamond Girl block with the Sawtooth Star. Large green Rising Stars surround burgundy, red, and rust Sawtooth Stars in a straight set to form an overall design.

Alternating Pieced Blocks

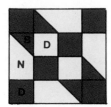
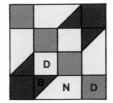

Block A   Block B

Dimensions: 64" x 80"

Measurements for patterns and borders include 1/4" seam allowance.

Materials: 45" wide yardage

Light fabric: 2 yds. assorted white, beige, cream prints

Dark fabric: 1 1/2 yds. assorted brown prints

Accent fabric for Block A: 1/2 yd. assorted rust prints

Accent fabric for Block B: 1/2 yd. assorted tan prints

Backing: 3 3/4 yds. fabric

Batting, binding, and thread to finish

Cutting:

Block A or B
  B: Cut 4 dark
  D: Cut 2 light
     Cut 2 dark
     Cut 4 accent
  N: Cut 2 light
     Cut 2 light R

Directions:

1. Cut and piece 40 blocks with coloration A and 40 with coloration B.

2. Set top together as shown, alternating Block A and Block B.

3. Add batting and backing, then quilt or tie.

4. Bind with bias strips.

Road to Oklahoma, by Nancy Mahoney, 1987, Seattle, Washington, 64" x 80". The star pattern emerges as blocks sewn in two different color variations are combined.

Dimensions: 64'' x 80''

Alternating Pieced Blocks

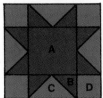
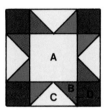

Sawtooth Star   Art Square

Half Blocks   Quarter Block

Dimensions: 84" x 100"

Measurements for patterns and borders include 1/4" seam allowance.

Materials: 45" wide yardage

Light fabric: 5/8 yd. assorted lavender prints
Medium fabric: 3 1/2 yds. assorted mauve prints
Dark fabric: 3 yds. assorted green prints
Border: 2 1/2 yds. green print
Backing: 5 3/4 yds. fabric
Batting, binding, and thread to finish

Cutting:

Sawtooth Star
  A: Cut 1 medium
  B: Cut 8 medium
  C: Cut 4 dark
  D: Cut 4 dark

Art Square:
  B: Cut 8 dark
  D: Cut 4 light
  K: Cut 1 light

Quarter Block:
  B: Cut 2 medium
      Cut 2 dark
  D: Cut 1 medium
      Cut 1 dark

Half Sawtooth Star
  B: Cut 4 medium
      Cut 2 dark
  C: Cut 1 dark
  D: Cut 2 dark
  F: Cut 1 medium

Half Art Square
  B: Cut 4 dark
  D: Cut 2 light
  L: Cut 1 light

Directions:

1. Cut and piece 32 Sawtooth Star blocks.

2. Cut and piece 31 Art Square blocks.

3. Cut and piece 18 Art Square half blocks, 14 Sawtooth Star half blocks, and 4 quarter blocks.

4. Set together top as shown, alternating Sawtooth Star and Art Square blocks, using appropriate half block to complete rows. Quarter blocks are used for corners in the top and bottom row.

5. Stitch 10 1/4" x 80 1/2" borders to each side.

6. Stitch 10 1/4" x 84" borders to top and bottom of quilt top.

7. Add batting and backing, then quilt or tie.

8. Bind with bias strips.

Variation I:
JANE'S QUILT

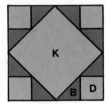
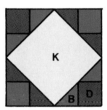

Sawtooth Star   Art Square

Half Blocks   Quarter Block

Dimensions: 38" x 38"

Alternate coloration results in a quilt resembling Hovering Hawks.

Jane's Quilt, by Nancy Martin, 1986, Seattle, Washington, 38" x 38". Anonymous quilter.

Dimensions: 84" x 100"

Blazing Sawtooth, by Nancy Martin, 1986, Seattle, Washington, 84'' x 100''. Lavender and green prints create a restful star design. Anonymous quilter.

Variation II:
OCEAN STARS

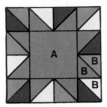 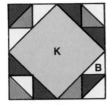 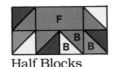  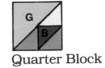

Split Sawtooth Star   Ocean Star   Half Blocks   Quarter Block

Dimensions: 61 1/2" x 61 1/2"

Ocean Stars can be made by substituting the Ocean Star block for the Art Square block.
A Split Sawtooth Star block is used.

Ocean Stars, by Nancy J. Martin, 1986, Seattle, Washington, 61 1/2" x 61 1/2". This variation of Blazing Sawtooth uses the Ocean Star block rather than Art Square to create a design similar to Ocean Waves. The slipcover fabric used in the pieced stars sets the color scheme for this pastel quilt. Subtle color variations make the stars disappear. Quilted by Freda Smith.

Pieced Blocks and Lattices

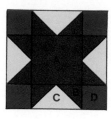  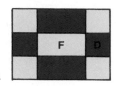

Lattice Section A

Sawtooth Star

Lattice Section B

Dimensions: 58" x 72"

Measurements for patterns and borders include 1/4" seam allowance.

Materials: 45" wide yardage

Light fabric: 1 1/2 yds. assorted beige, tan, gold prints
Medium fabric: 1 yd. assorted rust, cranberry, maroon prints
Dark fabric: 1 1/3 yds. assorted blue prints
Border: 1 7/8 yds. rust print
Backing: 3 1/4 yds. print
Batting, binding and thread to finish

Cutting:
Sawtooth Star:
  A: Cut 1 medium
  B: Cut 8 medium
  C: Cut 4 light
  D: Cut 4 dark

Lattice Section A:
  D: Cut 4 light
    Cut 5 dark
Lattice Section B:
  D: Cut 4 light
    Cut 2 dark
  F: Cut 1 light
    Cut 2 dark

Directions:

1. Cut and piece 20 Sawtooth Star blocks.

2. Cut and piece 12 Lattice Sections A and 31 Lattice Sections B.

3. Join 4 Sawtooth Star blocks with 3 Lattice Section B units to form a row. Piece together a total of 5 rows.

4. Alternate 3 Lattice Section A units with 4 Lattice Section B units to form lattice rows. Piece 4 of these lattice rows together.

5. Set together top as shown, alternating rows of Sawtooth Star blocks and lattice rows.

6. Stitch 4 1/4" x 64 1/2" borders to each side.

7. Stitch 4 1/4" x 58" borders to top and bottom of quilt top.

8. Add backing and batting, then quilt or tie.

9. Bind with bias strips.

Checkerboard Stars, by Nancy Martin, 1986, Seattle, Washington, 58" x 72". Judy Martin's design is pieced in a variation of the traditional red, white, and blue color scheme.

Dimensions: 58'' x 72''

Pieced Blocks and Lattices

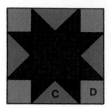

Sawtooth Star

Lattice Section A

Lattice Section B

Stardancer, by Marsha McCloskey, 1985, Seattle, Washington, 52" x 76".

Dimensions: 52" x 76"

Measurements for patterns and borders include 1/4" seam allowance.

Materials: 45" wide yardage

Light fabric: 1/2 yd. assorted taupe prints
Medium fabric: 1 1/4 yds. assorted pink prints
Dark fabric: 5/8 yd. assorted navy prints
Accent fabric 1: 3/4 yd. assorted burgundy prints
Border: 1 7/8 yds. fabric
Backing: 3 yds. fabric
Batting, binding, and thread to finish

Cutting:

Sawtooth Star:
  A: Cut 1 accent
  B: Cut 8 dark
  C: Cut 4 medium
  D: Cut 4 light

Lattice Section A:
  A: Cut 1 light
  B: Cut 4 dark
  C: Cut 2 medium

Lattice Section B:
  A: Cut 1 light

Directions:

1. Cut and piece 24 Sawtooth Star blocks.

2. Cut and piece 38 Lattice Sections A. Cut 15 Lattice Sections B.

3. Join 4 Sawtooth Star blocks with 3 Lattice Section A units to form a row. Piece together a total of 6 rows.

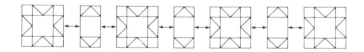

4. Alternate 3 Lattice Section B and 4 Lattice Section A units to form lattice rows. Piece 5 of these lattice rows together.

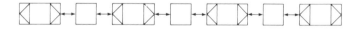

5. Set together top as shown, alternating rows of Sawtooth Star blocks and lattice rows.

6. Stitch 4 1/4" x 68 1/2" borders to each side.

7. Add 4 1/4" x 52" borders to top and bottom of quilt top.

8. Add batting and backing, then quilt or tie.

9. Bind with bias strips.

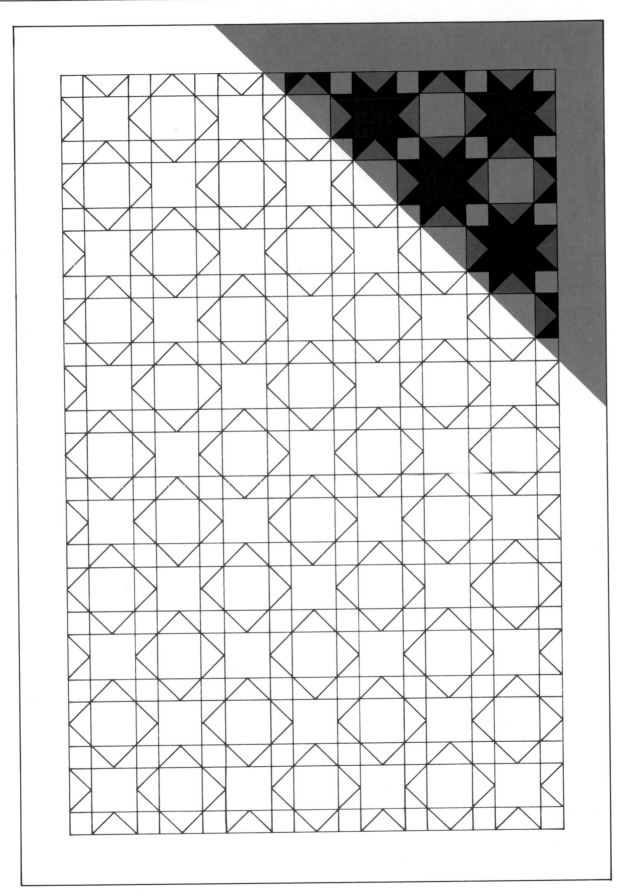

Dimensions: 52" x 74"

Rock Star, by Marsha McCloskey, 1985, Seattle, Washington, 52" x 76". The colors for this quilt were inspired by a geological tour through Hart's Pass in the Cascade Mountains. In late summer, the dusty red earth contrasted with the soft green sage and pine. Quilted by Freda Smith.

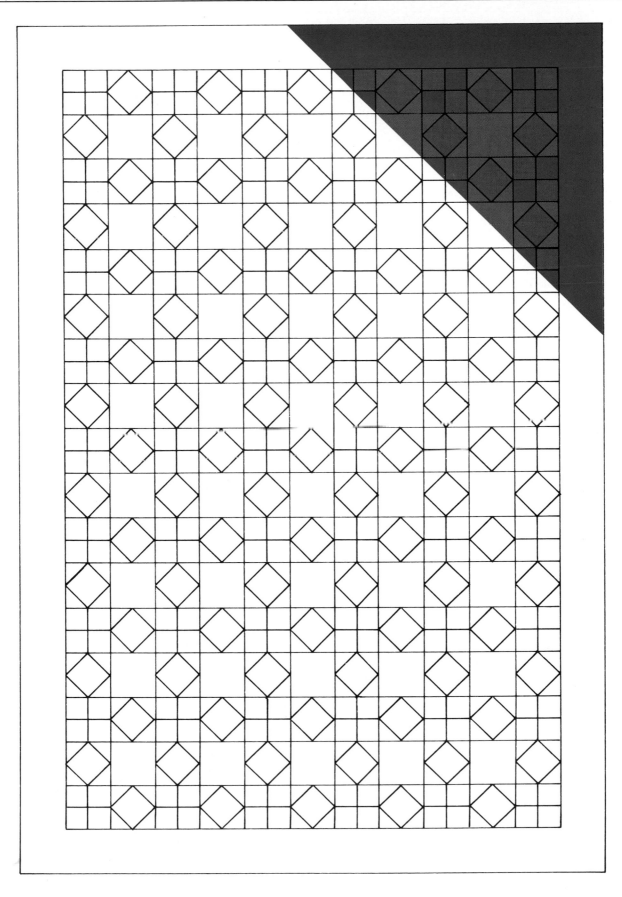

Dimensions: 52" x 76"

Allover Pattern

Unit A   Unit B   Unit C

Dimensions: 52" x 76"
Measurements for patterns and borders include 1/4"
seam allowance.

Materials: 45" wide yardage
Light fabric: 1 1/2 yds. assorted pink prints
Medium fabric: 1 1/2 yds. assorted green prints
Dark fabric: 1 1/2 yds. assorted brown prints
Border: 2 yds. brown fabric
Backing: 3 yds. fabric
Batting, binding, and thread to finish

Cutting:
A: Cut 1 light
B: Cut 4 light
D: Cut 2 medium
    Cut 2 dark
E: Cut 1 medium

Directions:
1. Cut and piece the following segments:
    40 Unit A, 93 Unit B, 54 Unit C

2. Set top together as shown, alternating rows.
    Row 1

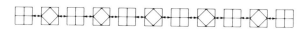

    Row 2

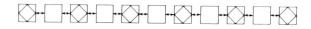

3. Stitch 4 1/4" x 68 1/2" borders to each side.

4. Stitch 4 1/4" x 52" borders to top and bottom of
quilt top.

5. Add backing and batting, then quilt or tie.

6. Bind with bias strips.

Allover Pattern

Unit A   Unit A   Unit B   Unit C

Dimensions: 52" x 76"

Measurements for patterns and borders include 1/4" seam allowance.

Materials: 45" wide yardage

Light fabric: 1 1/2 yds. white, light gray, beige prints
Medium fabric: 1 1/2 yds. assorted red, cranberry, rust, maroon prints
Dark fabric: 1 1/2 yds. gray, black prints
Border: 2 yds. fabric
Backing: 3 yds. fabric
Batting, binding and thread to finish

Cutting:

Unit A
  A: Cut 1 medium or
     Cut 1 dark

Unit B
  B: Cut 4 light
     Cut 2 medium
     Cut 2 dark

Unit C
  B: Cut 2 medium
     Cut 2 dark
  E: Cut 1 light

Directions:

1. Cut and piece the following segments:
     20 Unit A from medium fabric
     20 Unit A from dark fabric
     54 Unit B, 93 Unit C

2. Set top together as shown, alternating rows.

Row 1

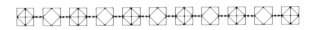

Row 2

Row 3

Row 4

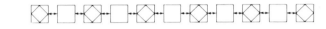

3. Stitch 4 1/4" x 68 1/2" borders to each side.

4. Stitch 4 1/4" x 52" borders to top and bottom of quilt top.

5. Add backing and batting, then quilt or tie.

6. Bind with bias strips.

Starlight, by Marsha McCloskey, 1985, Seattle, Washington, 52'' x 76''. Alternating black and red stars rest on a flowing background of white and gray prints. Quilted by Freda Smith.

Dimensions: 52" x 76"

Allover Pattern

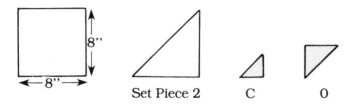

Unit A   Unit A   Unit B

Set Pieces

8"
←—8"—→

Set Piece 2   C   0

Border

Measurements for patterns and borders include 1/4" seam allowance.

Dimensions: 56" x 72 3/4"

Materials: 45" wide yardage
Light fabric: 2 1/2 yds. assorted white, cream prints
Medium fabric: 2 1/2 yds. assorted tan fabrics
Dark fabric: 2 1/2 yds. assorted deep pink prints
Border: 5/8 yd. assorted light pink fabrics
        5/8 yd. assorted dark pink fabrics
Backing: 3 1/4 yds. fabric
Batting, binding, and thread to finish

Cutting: (for entire quilt)
Unit A: Cut 12 dark
        Cut 6 medium

Unit B:
  B: Cut 8 dark
  C: Cut 4 light
Set Pieces for entire quilt:
  Set Piece 2: Cut 14 light
  8" x 8" block: Cut 17 light
  0: Cut 10 medium
  C: Cut 4 medium

Border:
  C: Cut 88 light pink
     Cut 88 dark pink

Directions:

1. Cut and piece the following segments: 18 Unit A and 48 Unit B.

2. Cut set pieces. Construct top alternating Unit B with Unit A or set pieces.

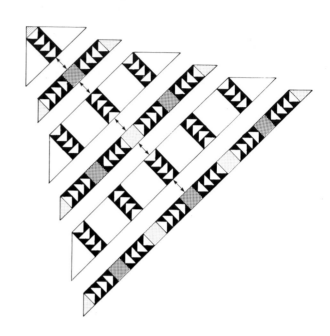

3. Piece 88 border units. See Fast Triangle Method on page 60.

4. Add a segment of 18 pieced triangles to top and bottom of quilt.

5. Add a segment of 26 pieced triangles to each side of quilt.

6. Add backing and batting, then quilt or tie.

7. Bind with bias strips.

Dimensions: 56" x 72 3/4"

Star Chase, by Marsha McCloskey, 1986, Seattle, Washington, 56 x 72 3/4''. This design was inspired by an antique quilt top. The star pattern is created as the geese fly into the center of the block. Barely contrasting shades of pink create a subtle Sawtooth border. Quilted by Freda Smith.

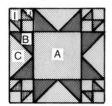

Twinkling Star

Dimensions: 37" x 53"

Measurements for patterns and borders include 1/4" seam allowance.

Materials: 45 inch wide yardage

Light fabric: 1 1/2 yds. assorted gray prints

Accent fabric: 1 yd. assorted red, maroon, rust, burgundy prints

Dark fabric: 1 yd. assorted navy prints

Border: 3/4 yd. navy fabric

Backing: 1/58 yds. fabric

Batting, binding, and thread to finish

Cutting:

A: Cut 1 light
B: Cut 8 dark
C: Cut 4 light
I: Cut 8 light
J: Cut 8 accent
   Cut 8 light

Border:
C: Cut 32 light gray
   Cut 68 accent
   Cut 28 dark gray
H: Cut 8 dark gray

Directions:

1. Cut and piece 15 Twinkling Star blocks

2. Set blocks together as pictured.

3. Piece inner border units

Side unit
Piece 2

Top or bottom unit
Piece 2

4. Piece outer border units.

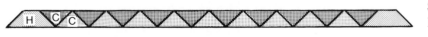
Side unit
Piece 2

Top or bottom unit
Piece 2

5. Cut two 3" x 55" strips for side borders and two 3" x 39" strips for top and bottom border.

6. Join corresponding pieced inner border, pieced outer border, and outside border to form a border segment for each side, top and bottom.

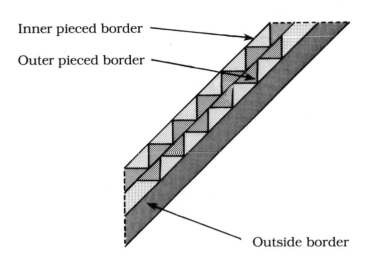

Inner pieced border

Outer pieced border

Outside border

7. Attach border to pieced section of the quilt, stopping 1/4" from outer edges. Back tack.

8. To complete corner, follow directions given on Mitering Corners on page 61.

9. Add backing and batting, then quilt or tie.

10. Bind with bias strips.

Twinkling Stars, by Marsha McCloskey, 1986, Seattle, Washington, 37" x 53". Small "twinkling stars" emerge at the corners when Twinkling Star blocks are sewn together. The pieced zig zag border adds excitement and movement to the design.

Detail: Twinkling Stars.

Dimensions: 37'' x 53''

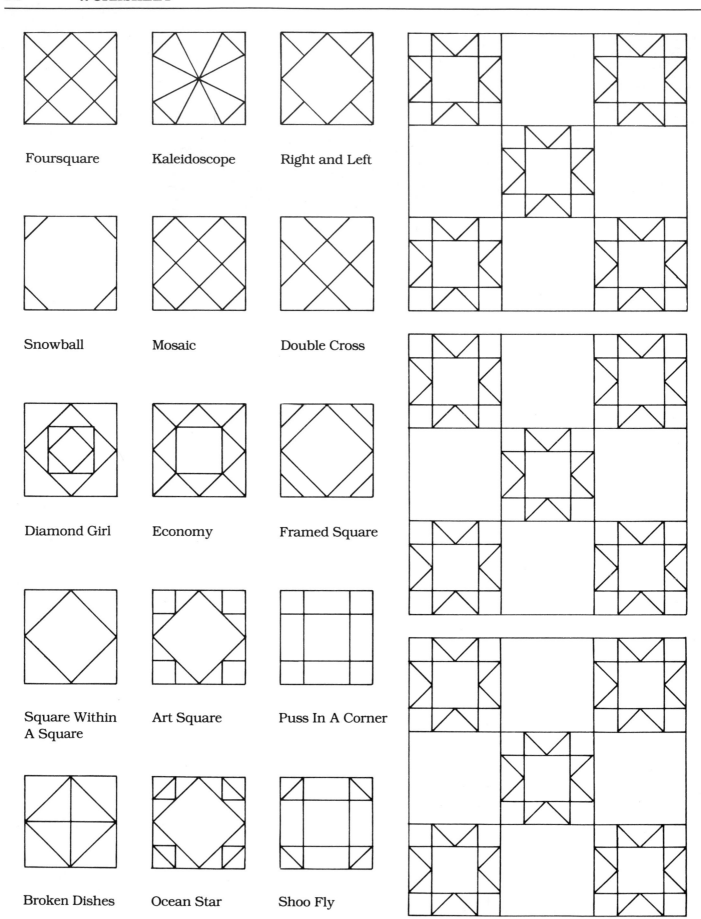

Foursquare

Kaleidoscope

Right and Left

Snowball

Mosaic

Double Cross

Diamond Girl

Economy

Framed Square

Square Within
A Square

Art Square

Puss In A Corner

Broken Dishes

Ocean Star

Shoo Fly

TEMPLATES

To make each unit block, you will need a set of pattern pieces or templates. Carefully trace the templates from the book onto graph paper or tracing paper. Trace accurately and transfer to the paper all information printed on the templates in the book.

Each template for the unit blocks is labeled with a letter. Cutting directions are provided with each quilt pattern. An "R" in a cutting notation means "reverse". The pieces are mirror images: cut the first number of pieces with the template face up and then flip it over face down to cut the remainder.

Templates have seam lines (broken lines) as well as cutting lines (solid lines). Grainlines are for the lengthwise or crosswise grain and are shown with an arrow on each piece. Fold lines indicate where half templates are given due to space limitations. Complete the other half of the pattern when you make larger templates. Consult the Glossary of Techniques on pages 58 - 63 for complete directions on quiltmaking techniques.

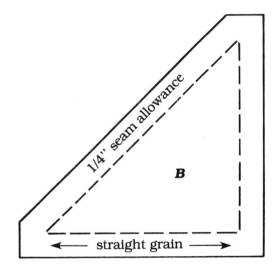

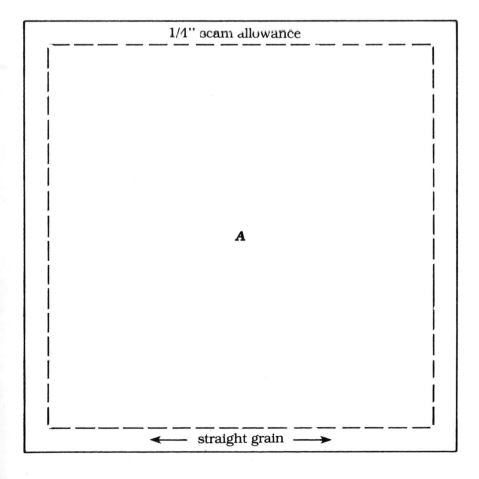

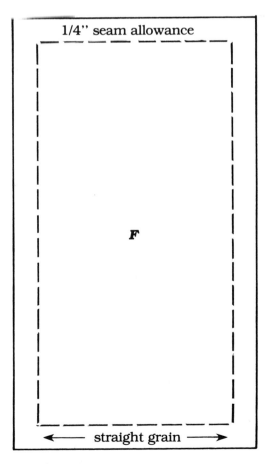

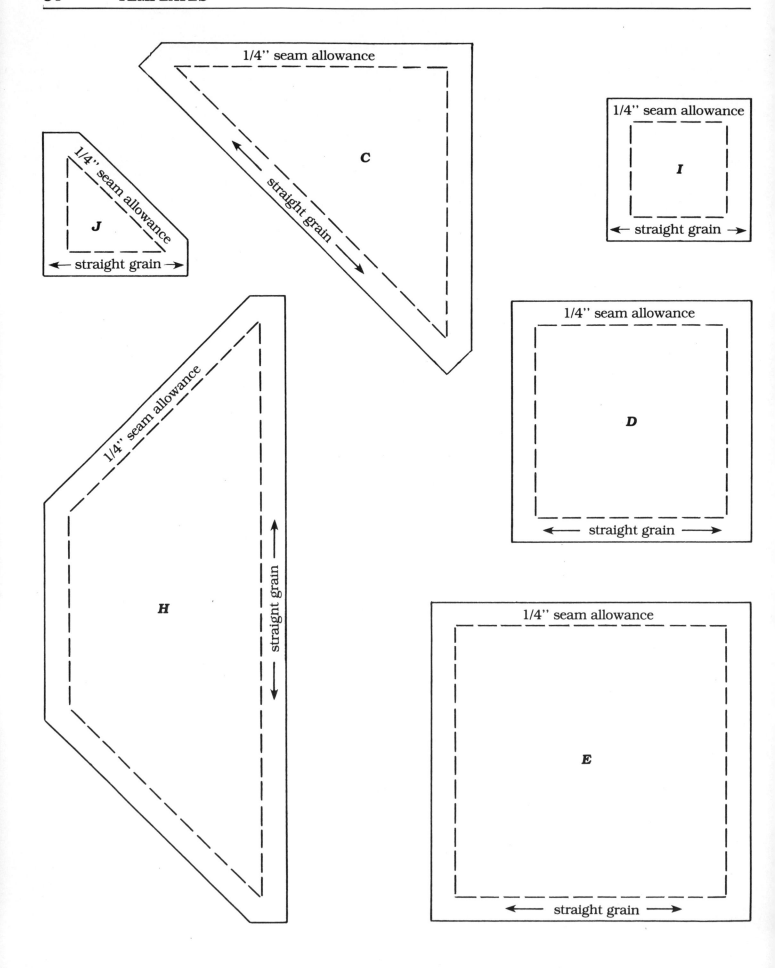

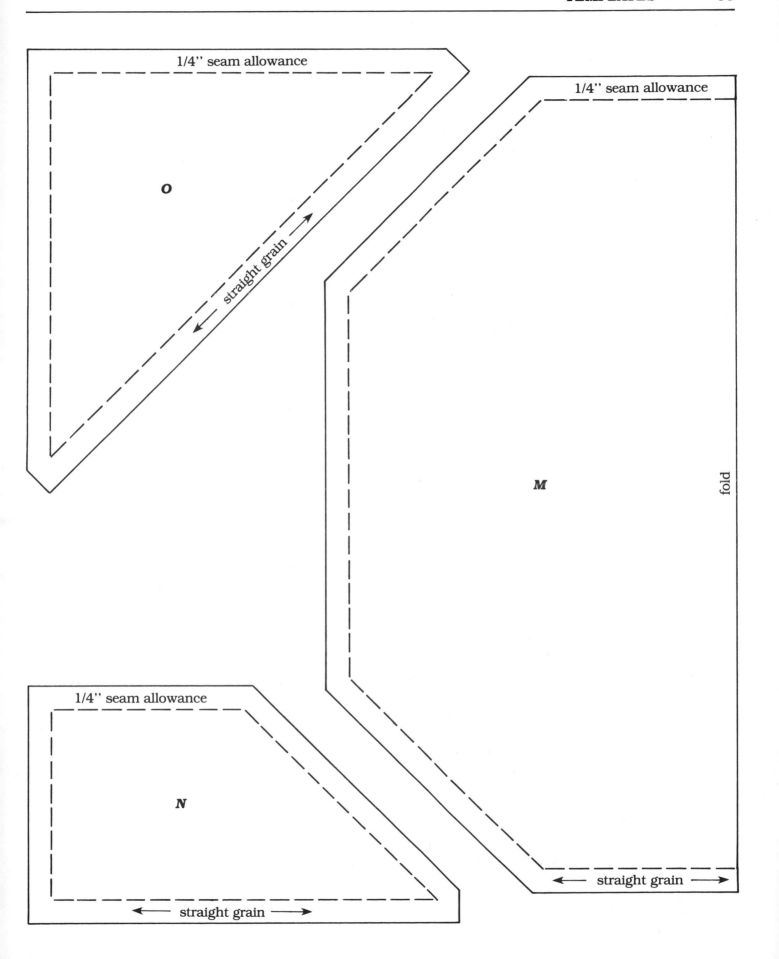

1/4'' seam allowance

O

straight grain

1/4'' seam allowance

M

fold

1/4'' seam allowance

N

← straight grain →

← straight grain →

NOTE: Smaller pieces overlap larger pieces, so be sure to include the entire template, including the space covered by the smaller piece, when you make the larger template.

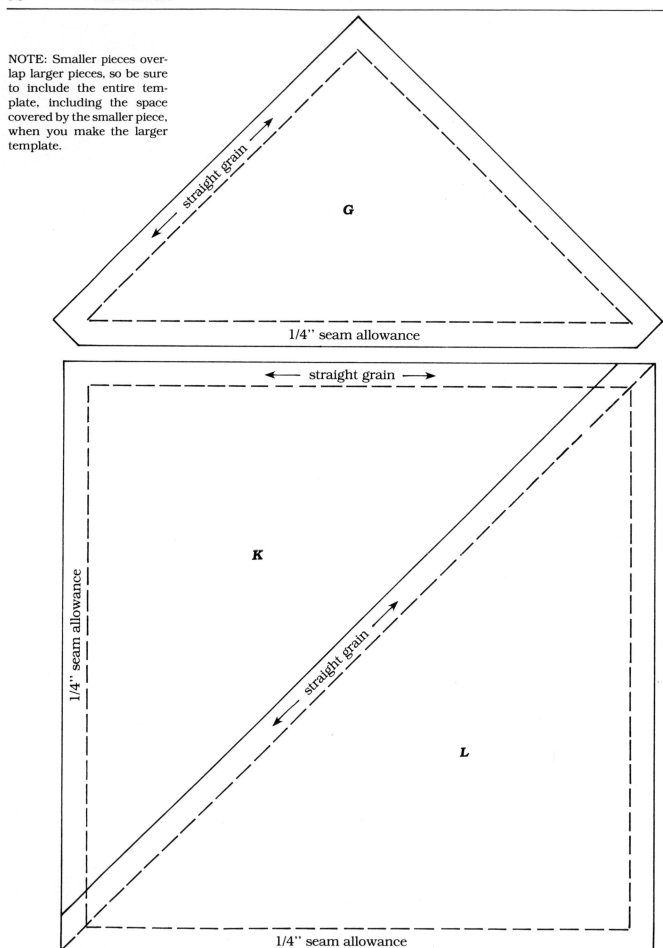

G

straight grain

1/4" seam allowance

straight grain

K

1/4" seam allowance

straight grain

L

1/4" seam allowance

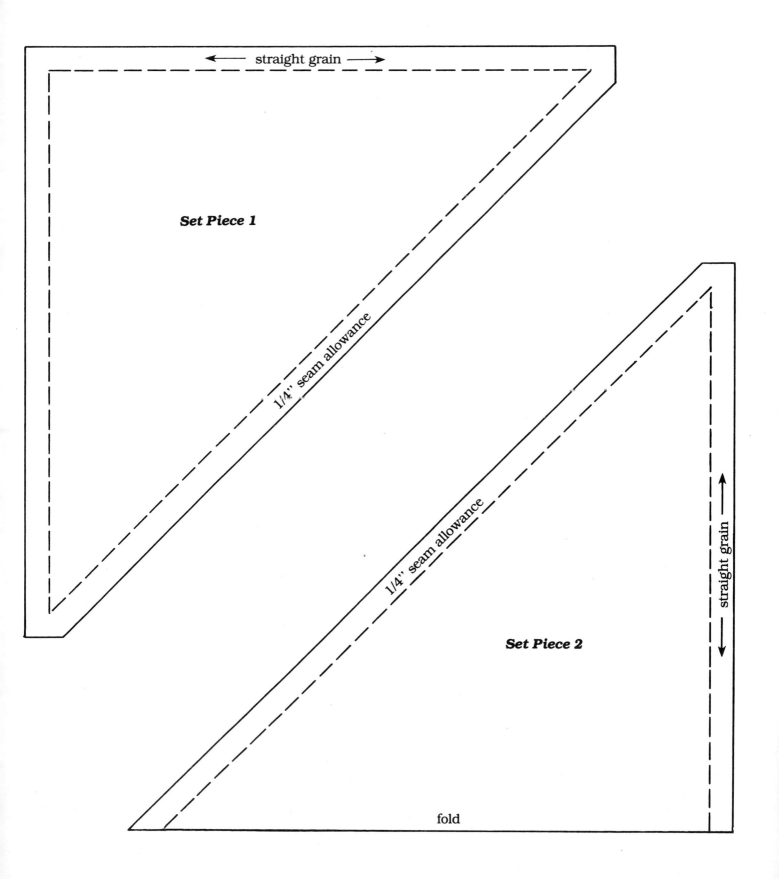

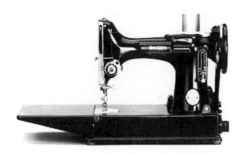

Tools and Supplies

Drawing Supplies: Graph paper in a 1/8" grid and colored pencils for drawing quilt plans and sketching design ideas.

Rulers: I use two rulers; both are clear plastic with a red grid of 1/8" squares. A short ruler is for drawing quilt designs on graph paper; a longer one, 2" wide and 18" long, is for drafting designs full size, making templates, and measuring and marking borders and quilting lines. If your local quilt shop doesn't carry them, try a stationery store or any place that carries drafting or art supplies. Another useful tool is a 12" plastic 45°/90° right angle.

Scissors: You will need scissors for paper, a good sharp pair for cutting fabric only, and possibly a little pair for snipping threads. If your fabric scissors are dull, have them sharpened. If they are close to "dead," invest in a new pair. It's worth it.

Template Material: To make templates, you will need graph paper or tracing paper, lightweight posterboard (manila file folders are good) or plastic, and a glue stick.

Markers: Most marking on fabric can be done with a regular #2 lead pencil and a white dressmaker's pencil. Keep them sharp. There is a blue felt-tip marking pen available that is water erasable; it works especially well for marking quilting designs. (When you no longer need the lines for guides, spray them with cool water and the blue marks will disappear.) Ask the salespeople at a local fabric or quilt shop about the different kinds of marking pens available.

Sewing Machine: It needn't be fancy. All you need is an evenly locking straight stitch. Whatever kind of sewing machine you have, get to know it and how it runs. If it needs servicing, have it done, or get out the manual and do it yourself. Replace the old needle with a new one. Often, if your machine has a zigzag stitch, it will have a throat plate with an oblong hole for the needle to pass through. You might want to replace this plate with one that has a little round hole for straight stitching. This will help eliminate problems you might have with the edges of fabrics being fed into the hole by the action of the feed dog.

Needles: A supply of new sewing machine needles for light to medium weight cottons is necessary. You'll also need an assortment of Sharps for handwork and quilting needles (Between #8, #9, or #10) if you plan to hand quilt.

Pins: Multicolored glass or plastic-headed pins are generally longer, stronger, and easier to see and hold than regular dressmaker's pins.

Iron and Ironing Board: A shot of steam is useful.

Seam Ripper: I always keep one handy.

Cutting

Study the design and templates. Determine the number of pieces to cut of each shape and each fabric. Trim the selvage from the fabric before you begin cutting. When one fabric is to be used both for borders and in the unit block designs, cut the borders first and the smaller pieces from what is left over (see Borders on page 61).

At the ironing board, press and fold the fabric so that one, two or four layers can be cut at one time (except for linear prints such as stripes and checks that should be cut one at a time). Fold the fabric so that each piece will be cut on the straight grain.

Position stiffened templates on the fabric so the arrows match the straight grain of the fabric. With a sharp pencil (white for dark fabrics, lead for light ones), trace around the template on the fabric. This is the cutting line. Cut just inside this line to most accurately duplicate the template.

In machine piecing, there are no drawn lines to guide your sewing. The seamline is 1/4" from the cut edge of the fabric, so this outside edge must be precisely cut to ensure accurate sewing.

Machine Piecing

For machine piecing, use white or neutral thread as light in color as the lightest fabric in the project. Use a dark neutral thread for piecing dark solids. It is easier to work with 100% cotton thread on some machines. Check your needle. If it is dull, burred or bent, replace it with a fresh one.

Sew exact 1/4" seams. To determine the 1/4" seam allowance on your machine, place a template under the presser foot and gently lower the needle onto the seamline. The distance from the needle to the edge of the template is 1/4". Lay a piece of masking tape at the edge of the template to act as the 1/4" mark; use the edge as a guide. Stitch length should be set at 10-12 stitches per inch. For most of the sewing in this book, sew from cut edge to cut edge (exceptions will be noted). Backtack, if you wish, although it is really not necessary as each seam will be crossed and held by another.

Use chain piecing whenever possible to save time and thread. To chain piece, sew one seam, but do not lift the presser foot. Do not take the piece out of the sewing machine and do not cut the thread. Instead, set up the next seam to be sewn and stitch as you did the first. There will be a little twist of thread between the two pieces. Sew all the seams you can at one time in this way, then remove the "chain". Clip the threads.

Chain piecing

Press the seam allowances to one side, toward the darker fabric when possible. Avoid too much ironing as you sew because it tends to stretch biases and distort fabric shapes.

To piece a block, sew the smallest pieces together first to form units. Join smaller units to form larger ones until the block is complete.

Short seams need not be pinned unless matching is involved, or the seam is longer than 4". Keep pins away from the seamline. Sewing over pins tends to burr the needle and makes it hard to be accurate in tight places.

Here are five matching techniques that can be helpful in many different piecing situations.

1. Opposing Seams: When stitching one seamed unit to another, press seam allowances on the seam that needs to match in opposite directions. The two "opposing" seams will hold each other in place and evenly distribute the bulk. Plan pressing to take advantage of opposing seams.

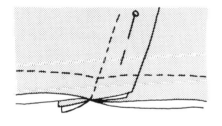

2. Positioning Pin: A pin, carefully pushed straight through two points that need to match and pulled tight, will establish the proper point of matching. Pin the seam normally and remove the positioning pin before stitching.

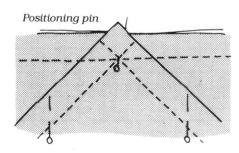

Positioning pin

3. The "X": When triangles are pieced, stitches will form an "X" at the next seamline. Stitch through the center of the "X" to make sure the points on the sewn triangles will not be chopped off.

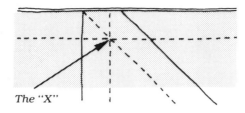

The "X"

4. Easing: When two pieces to be sewn together are supposed to match but instead are slightly different lengths, pin the points to match and stitch with the shorter piece on top. The feed dog eases the fullness of the bottom piece.

5. Making Eight Points Come Together: To make eight points come together crisply as needed in the Whirlygig block and many others, follow these three steps: First, chain piece light and dark triangles together to form four squares. Press each seam towards the dark. Second, make two halves of the pinwheel by sewing two square units together as shown. Match using opposing diagonal seams. Press each new seam towards the dark. Third, sew the center seam. Match using positioning pin and opposing seams. Stitch exactly through the "X".

Basic Star Assembly

Triangles are pieced first to form units. These units are then joined with squares into rows. Press seams of units as shown. This will ensure flat seam intersections and aid in piecing blocks together.

Stitch rows together into blocks. Press as shown.

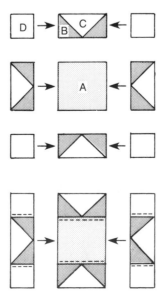

Template-Free Techniques

Special tools and template-free techniques will help to speed the piecing process and ensure accuracy. For more information on template-free techniques, see *Template-Free Quiltmaking* by Trudie Hughes and *More Template-Free Quiltmaking* by Trudie Hughes, published by That Patchwork Place, Inc., Bothell, Wa.

Tools:

Rotary Cutter and Mat: A large rotary cutter will enable you to quickly cut strips and pieces without templates. A mat with a rough finish will hold the fabric in place and protect both the blade and the table on which you are cutting.

Cutting Guides: You will need a ruler for measuring and to guide the rotary cutter. The Rotary Rule™, made from 1/4" Plexiglas™, includes markings for 45° and 60° angles, guidelines for use in subcutting strips, plus the standard measurements. When cutting individual quilt pieces, a smaller guide such as the Bias Square™ is helpful.

All pieces are cut with the 1/4" seam allowance included. If accurate 1/4" seams are sewn by machine, there is no need to mark stitching lines.

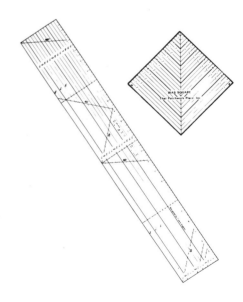

* The ROTARY RULE™ is available through Patched Works, 13330 Watertown Plank Rd., Elm Grove, Wisconsin 53122. The Bias Square™ is available through That Patchwork Place, Inc., P.O. Box 118, Bothell, QA 98041.

Four Patch and Ninepatch Units

Long fabric strips are sewn together in units called strata and then subcut into shorter portions; the small units are then combined to form Four Patch Units or Ninepatch Units.

It is best to cut strips from the lengthwise grain of the fabric. When it is necessary to use the cross-grain to get the required length, be sure to straighten the fabric so strips will be cut exactly on-grain.

Press the fabric well before cutting strips. The accuracy of the piecing will depend largely on how carefully fabric, strips, and seams are pressed.

To determine the width to cut strips, add a 1/4" seam allowance to each side of the finished strip. For example, if the finished dimension of the piece will be 1", cut 1 1/2" strips. Stack the fabric before marking and cutting so two or four layers can be cut at one time. Cut with a rotary cutter. Try to be accurate; speed-piecing does not mean sloppy piecing.

Sew long strips together with 1/4" seam allowances, but wait to press until all the strips in the unit have been sewn. Press seam allowances toward the darker fabric, and press from the right side of the work so the fabric won't pleat along the seam lines.

Four Patch Units

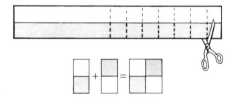

Ninepatch Units

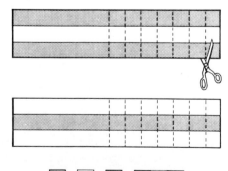

Bias-Strip Piecing

Use bias-strip piecing when working with triangles. Half-square triangles, as well as many other shapes, can be cut using this method. When these half-square triangles are used in a Variable Star block there will be an extra seam. In a design using many print fabrics, this is usually not noticeable.

Half-square triangles

 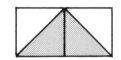

Variable Star block using half-square triangles

Use the rotary cutter and cutting guide to cut two bias strips of fabric, one dark and one light. Fabric may be layered so that both light and dark strips are cut at the same time.

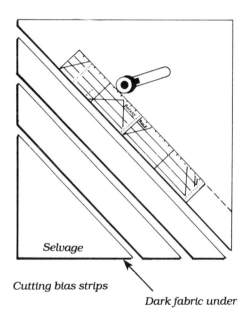

Cutting bias strips

Selvage

Dark fabric under

To determine the width of the bias strips, measure the square template to be used from corner to corner (including seam allowances) on the diagonal. Add 3" and divide by 2.

$$\frac{X'' + 3''}{2} = \text{width of each bias strip}$$

Sew the strips together on the long bias edge, using 1/4" seam allowance. Press seams open or toward the dark fabric.

Bias strips

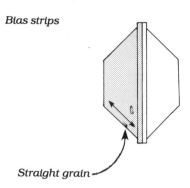

Straight grain

Align 45° angle marking of cutting guide with seamline. Cut first two sides of square. Measure distance from cut edge to opposite side of square and cut. Measure and cut four sides in the same manner.

Cut first two sides

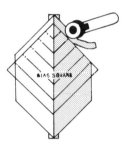

Cut opposite two sides

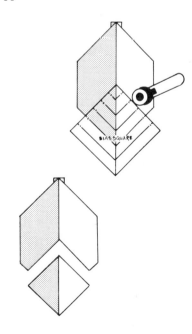

Always align 45° angle marking with seamline before you cut the next square. This ensures accuracy.

Odd-Size Pieces

Occasionally you will need to cut a small odd size square or rectangle for which there is no marking on your cutting guide. I make an accurate paper template (including 1/4" seam allowance) and tape it to the top of the Bias Square™. You now have the correct alignment for cutting strips or squares.

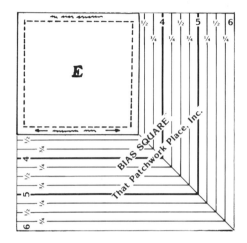

Setting the Quilt Together

When all of the blocks are pieced, you are ready to "set" the quilt top together, following a setting plan. First stitch together blocks or blocks and lattices into rows, using 1/4" seams. Then stitch together rows of blocks or blocks and lattice strips. Setting sequences are shown in diagrams.

When the center portion is pieced together, borders can then be added to the quilt.

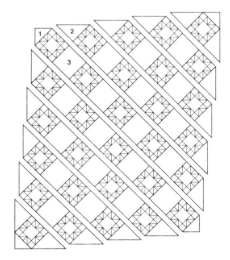

Assembly sequence of diagonally set quilt.

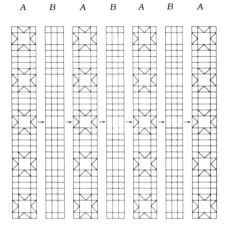

Assembly sequence with lattices

Borders

Borders function as a frame for a quilt design. For plain borders with straight sewn corners, first sew borders to the long sides of the quilt, then to the width. Striped fabrics make lovely quilt borders, but the corner must be mitered to make the design turn the corner gracefully. Mitered corners are not difficult to do and are worth the effort in some design situations. Miter corners when using stripes of multiple plain borders.

You will need to buy fabric the length of the longest outside border plus about 4" to allow for shrinkage. It is often wise when cutting border strips to leave them 3" to 4" longer than the length given in the pattern. When the actual dimensions of the quilt top are known, the border strips can be trimmed to fit.

Border strips should always be cut from yardage before the templates, ensuring that you have continuous yardage. If you need to piece border strips, seams should be pressed open and placed in the center of each side of the quilt for minimum visibility. If you are using a striped border, it is best not to piece it.

Always measure the length and width through the center of the quilt top to determine border dimensions. (Outside edges may have stretched or distorted.) Pin borders to quilt top evenly easing in any fullness on top or border. Stitch together in a 1/4" seam.

Mitering Corners

1. Prepare the borders. Determine the finished outside dimensions of your quilt. Cut the borders this length plus 1/2" for seam allowances. When using a striped fabric for the borders, make sure the design on all four borders is cut the same way. Multiple borders should be sewn together and the resulting "striped" units treated as a single border for mitering.

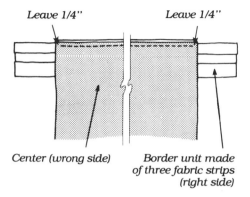

Center (wrong side)   *Border unit made of three fabric strips (right side)*

2. To attach the border to the pieced section of the quilt, center each border on a side so the ends extend equally on either side of the center section. Using a 1/4" seam allowance, sew the border to the center, leaving 1/4" unsewn at the beginning and end of the stitching line. Press the seam allowances toward the border.

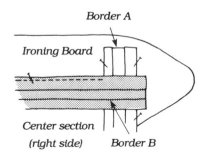

3. Arrange the first corner to be mitered on the ironing board as illustrated. Press the corner flat and straight. To prevent it from slipping, pin the quilt to the ironing board. Following the illustration, turn border "B" right side up, folding the corner to be mitered under at a 45° angle.

Match the raw edges underneath with those of border "A". Fuss with it until it looks good. The stripes and border designs should meet. Check the squareness of the corner with a right angle. Press the fold. This will be the sewing line. Pin the borders together to prevent shifting and unpin the piece from the board. Turn wrong side out and pin along the fold line, readjusting if necessary to match the designs.

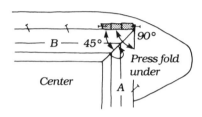

4. Machine baste from the inside to the outside corner on the fold line, leaving 1/4" at the beginning unsewn. Check for accuracy. If it is right, sew again with a regular stitch. Backtack at the beginning and end of the stitching line. (After you have mitered several times, the basting step ceases to be necessary.) Trim the excess fabric 1/4" along the mitered seam. Press this seam open. Press the other seams to the outside.

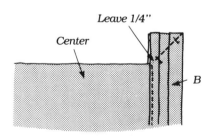

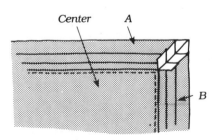

Preparing to Quilt

Marking

In most cases, before you quilt, the quilt top must be marked with lines to guide stitching. Where you place the quilting lines will depend on the patchwork design, the type of batting used, and how much quilting you want to do.

Try to avoid quilting too close to the seam lines, where the bulk of seam allowances might slow you down or make the stitches uneven. Also keep in mind that the purpose of quilting, besides its aesthetic value, is to securely hold the three layers together. Don't leave large areas unquilted.

Thoroughly press the quilt top and mark it, before it is assembled with the batting and backing. You will need marking pencils, a long ruler or yardstick, stencils or templates for quilting motifs, and a smooth, clean, hard surface on which to work. Use a sharp marking pencil and lightly mark the quilting lines on the fabric. No matter what kind of marking tool is used, light lines will be easier to remove than heavy ones.

Backing

A single length of 45"-wide fabric can often be used for backing small quilts. To be safe, plan on a usable width of only 42" after shrinkage and cutting off selvages. For larger quilts, two lengths of fabric will have to be sewn together to get one large enough.

Cut the backing 1" larger than the quilt top all the way around. Press thoroughly with seams open. Lay the backing face down on a large, clean, flat surface. With masking tape, tape the backing down (without stretching) to keep it smooth and flat while you are working with the other layers.

Batting

Batting is the filler in a quilt or comforter. Thick batting is used in comforters that are tied. If you plan to quilt, use thin batting and quilt by hand.

Thin batting comes in 100% polyester, 100% cotton, and a cotton-polyester (80%-20%) combination. All cotton batting requires close quilting to prevent shifting and separating in the wash. Most old quilts have cotton batting and are rather flat. Cotton is a good natural fiber that lasts well and is compatible with cotton and cotton-blend fabrics.

Less quilting is required on 100% polyester batting. If polyester batting is glazed or bonded, it is easy to work with, won't pull apart, and has more loft than cotton. Some polyester batting, however, has a tendency to "beard." This "fiber migration" (the small white polyester fibers creep to the quilt's surface between the threads in the fabric) happens mostly when polyester blends are used instead of 100% cotton fabrics. The cotton-polyester combination batting is supposed to combine the best features of the two fibers. A single layer of preshrunk cotton flannel can be used for filler instead of batting. The quilt will be very flat, and the quilting stitches highly visible.

Assembling the Layers

Center the freshly ironed and marked quilt top on top of the batting, face up. Starting in the middle, pin baste the three layers together while gently smoothing out fullness to the sides and corners. Take care not to distort the straight lines of the quilt design and the borders.

After pinning, baste the layers together with needle and light-colored thread. Start in the middle and make a line of large stitches to each corner to form a large X. Continue basting in a grid of parallel lines 6" to 8" apart. Finish with a row of basting around the outside edges. Quilts to be quilted with a hoop or on your lap will be handled more than those quilted on a frame; therefore, they will require more basting.

After basting, remove the pins. Now you are ready to quilt.

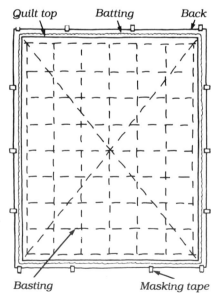

Hand Quilting

To quilt by hand, you will need quilting thread, quilting needles, small scissors, a thimble, and perhaps a balloon or large rubber band to help grasp the needle if it gets stuck. Quilt on a frame, a large hoop, or just on your lap or a table. Use a single strand of quilting thread not longer than 18". Make a small single knot in the end of the thread. The quilting stitch is a small running stitch that goes through all three layers of the quilt. Take two, three, or even four stitches at a time if you can keep them even. When crossing seams, you might find it necessary to "hunt and peck" one stitch at a time.

To begin, insert the needle in the top layer about 3/4" from the point you want to start stitching. Pull the needle out at the starting point and gently tug at the knot until it pops through the fabric and is buried in the batting. Make a backstitch and begin quilting. Stitches should be tiny (8 to 10 per inch is good), even, and straight. At first, concentrate on even and straight, tiny will come with practice.

When you come almost to the end of the thread, make a single knot fairly close to the fabric. Make a backstitch to bury the knot in the batting. Run the thread off through the batting and out the quilt top. Snip it off. The first and last stitches look different from the running stitches between. To make them less noticeable, start and stop where quilting lines cross each other or at seam joints.

Hand quilting stitch

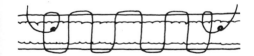

Binding

Bias Strips

To find the true bias, bring one side of fabric to the adjacent side and press. Using a rotary cutter and mat, cut 2 1/4" wide strips along the bias. Use pressed crease as a guideline.

Seam ends together to make a continuous long strip. Fold fabric in half lengthwise and press. This will give you a double layer of bias binding. After sewing, both seam allowances will be on the front of the quilt and the fold with no seam allowance will be on the back.

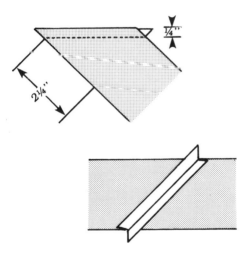

Binding the Edges

After quilting, trim excess batting and backing even with the edge of the quilt top. A rotary cutter and long ruler will ensure accurate straight edges. Baste all three layers together if basting from hand quilting is not still in place.

Directions:

1. Using a 1/4" seam allowance, sew the binding strips to the front of the quilt, sewing through all layers. Be careful not to stretch the bias or the quilt edge as you sew. Stitch until you reach the seam line point at the corner. Backstitch; cut threads.

2. Turn quilt to prepare for sewing along the next edge. Fold the binding away from the quilt as shown, then fold again to place binding along edge of quilt. (This fold creates an angled pleat at the corner.)

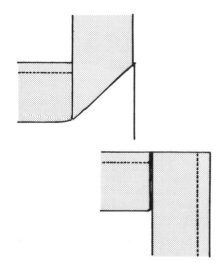

3. Stitch from the fold of the binding to the seam line of the adjacent edge. Backstitch; cut threads. Fold binding as in step 2, and continue around edge.

4. Join the beginning and ending of the binding strip, or plan to hand sew one end to overlap the other.

5. Turn binding to the back side, and blindstitch in place. At each corner, fold binding in the sequence shown to form a miter on the back of quilt.

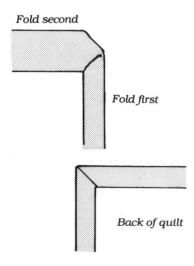

Fold second

Fold first

Back of quilt

BIBLIOGRAPHY

Carroll, Amy, ed. *Patchwork and Applique.* New York: Ballantine Books, 1981.

Finley, Ruth E. *Old Patchwork Quilts and the Woman Who Made Them.* Newton Center, Mass.: Charles T. Branford., Co., 1983.

"Great American Classics—The Variable Star." *Quilter's Newsletter Magazine,* February 1983, p. 24.

Hall, Carrie A. and Kretsinger, Rose G. *The Romance of the Patchwork Quilt.* New York: Dover Publications, Inc, 1988.

Holstein, Jonathan. *The Pieced Quilt: An American Design Tradition.* Greenwich, Conn.: New York Graphic Society, Ltd., 1973.

Horton, Roberta. *Calico and Beyond: The Use of Patterned Fabric in Quilts.* Lafayette, Calif.: C & T Publishing, 1986.

Martin, Judy. *Patchworkbook.* New York: Dover Publications, Inc., 1993.

Martin, Nancy. *Pieces of the Past.* Bothell, Wash.: That Patchwork Place, Inc., 1986.

McCloskey, Marsha R. *Small Quilts.* Bothell, Wash.: That Patchwork Place, Inc., 1982.

McKim, Ruby. *101 Patchwork Patterns.* New York: Dover Publications, Inc., 1962.

Nelson, Cyril I. and Houck, Carter. *The Quilt Engagement Calendar Treasury.* New York: E.P. Dutton, Inc., 1982.

Peto, Florence. *Historic Quilts.* New York: The American Historical Company, Inc., 1939.